The Wonders of Science

by Melvin Berger
illustrated by G. Brian Karas

SCHOLASTIC INC.

New York Toronto London Auckland Sydney

ISBN 0-590-43472-1
Text copyright © 1991 by Melvin Berger.
Illustrations copyright © 1991 by Scholastic Inc.
All rights reserved. Published by Scholastic Inc.

12 11 10 9   4 5 6/9

Printed in the U.S.A.   40

First Scholastic printing, March 1991

CONTENTS

WONDERS OF SOUND

Listen! What do you hear?
- People talking?
- Someone strumming on a guitar?
- A radio, TV, or stereo playing?
- The phone ringing?
- Cars driving by?
- A plane passing overhead?
- Raindrops hitting the windows?

You hear all sorts of sounds.

What Is Sound?

Here's how you can find out. Stretch a rubber band. Make it good and tight. Now keep your eye on the rubber band as you pluck it.

What do you see? The rubber band is shaking back and forth very fast.

What do you hear? A sound. A low, soft ping!

The very fast shaking back and forth of the rubber band makes the ping sound.

All sound is caused by the very fast shaking back and forth of some object. Fast shaking is called *vibration*. Vibrating objects make sounds.

WONDER FACT: All sounds are made by vibrating objects.

Each time you talk, play a musical instrument, or turn on the TV you make something vibrate. The bell of the telephone, the car motor, the plane engine — they all vibrate. When raindrops hit a window they make the glass vibrate. And the vibrations make the sound.

WONDER FACT: Bees buzz as their wings beat up and down. Crickets chirp by rubbing their legs together to make them vibrate. Dolphins make clicking sounds when the air vibrates as it goes through their blowholes.

You can feel the vibrations that make a sound. Hold your hand lightly on the front of your throat. Talk out loud — count to ten, sing a song, tell a joke. The quivering that you feel is the vibrations inside your throat.

When you speak you are breathing out. Your breath makes the vocal cords in your throat vibrate. And these vibrations produce the sound of your voice.

Rest your hand on a radio or stereo that is playing loudly. Move your hand around.

You'll feel vibrations there, too. The speaker part of the radio or stereo vibrates and makes the sound.

Now you know that all sound is vibration. But how does sound get from one place to another?

Sound Travels

When you make a sound, the vibrations go out in all directions. Anyone who is nearby hears it.

The vibrations travel as *sound waves*. Sound waves move through the air much as waves move through water.

Toss a pebble into the center of a pond or rain puddle. Watch the waves spread out in bigger and bigger circles. This is how sound waves move through the air.

But sound waves are different from water waves in one important way. You can see water waves. But you can't see sound waves in the air. You only know that they are there because you can hear the sound coming from the vibrating object.

WONDER FACT: The loudest sound ever heard on earth was made by the eruption of the volcano Krakatoa in 1883. The sound was so powerful that it was heard 3,000 miles away.

Sound waves get weaker and weaker as they move through the air. Stand close to a radio and the sound is loud. Move away and it gets softer. When the sound comes from very far away, it may be too soft to hear at all.

Go with a friend to a quiet street or park. Talk to each other in normal voices. Then start to back away from each other. Keep talking. Stop when you can no longer hear what your friend is saying. Measure the distance between the two of you. You're probably about two hundred yards apart.

Two hundred yards is twice the length of a football field. It is the distance that the sounds of normal speech will travel through air.

WONDER FACT: Some people on the Canary Islands speak a special whistling language called *silbo*. It can be heard up to five miles away.

The Speed of Sound

Clap your hands. It seems that you hear the clap instantly. But really the sound took a fraction of a second to travel from your hands to your ears.

WONDER FACT: Sound travels through air at a speed of 740 miles an hour.

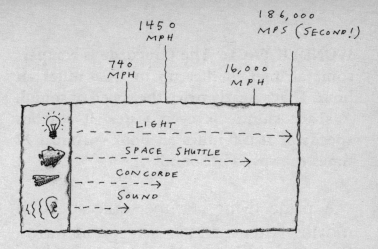

Even though sound travels very fast, light travels even faster. Light moves at 186,000 miles a *second*. That's nearly 700 million miles an hour! Or, almost a million times faster than sound!

Because light travels so much faster than sound, in a large baseball stadium you sometimes *see* the batter hit the ball before you *hear* the sound. Or, if you watch someone hammering from far away, you *see* the hammer strike before you *hear* the sound.

Many airplanes and all rockets can actually fly faster than sound. Anything that flies faster than sound is called *supersonic*.

WONDER FACT: The Concorde is a supersonic airliner. It flies up to 1,450 miles an hour. That's nearly twice the speed of sound. A space shuttle is even faster. It reaches speeds of 16,000 miles an hour — almost 22 times the speed of sound!

A plane flying at supersonic speed is moving faster than its own sound waves. It pushes its sound waves ahead of it. This produces a loud *bang!* The sound is called a *sonic boom*.

Hearing Sounds

Someone in the next room slams a door. You hear the sound. It makes you jump. But how does the sound reach your ears?

The slamming door makes the air around it vibrate. The vibrations form a sound wave in the air. The sound wave travels from the door to your ear.

Inside your ear is a thin, tight piece of tissue. Since it looks like a tiny drum it is called the *eardrum*.

The sound wave sets your eardrum vibrating. From the eardrum, the vibrations pass into your inner ear. Here the vibrations are changed into something like electrical signals.

These electrical signals zip through your nerves. They go straight to your brain. And your brain lets you know that a door was slammed shut.

Sound waves can pass through many different materials, as well as air. Wood, metal, earth, and water, all carry sound waves.

WONDER FACT: When hunting, American Indians used to hold one ear to the ground and listen. Sound waves passing through the earth let them hear the hoofbeats of far-off animals.

Stretch your arm out on a table. Scratch the tabletop with your fingernails. You'll hear a very soft sound. Now scratch the tabletop again. But this time rest your ear on the table. The sound is louder when it passes to your ear through the solid tabletop.

WONDER FACT: Sound moves faster through solids and liquids than through the air.

Water is a liquid. Sound moves through water about four times as fast as it moves through air.

Steel is a solid. Sound travels through steel fifteen times as fast as through air!

You can hear sound travel through string in a homemade telephone.

Stretch a long string fastened to the bottoms of two tin cans. Keep the string tight.

Speak into one can. This makes the string vibrate. The words you say can be heard in the other can.

Loud and Soft

Some sounds are louder than others. You can make both loud sounds and soft sounds. Clap your hands together as hard as you can. The sound is very loud.

Now gently tap your hands together. The sound is much softer. When you hit, rub, pluck, or blow softly, the vibrations are smaller. There is less sound.

Here's another way to make sounds softer. Hit a table hard with a wooden ruler or pencil. Listen to the sound. Now put a whole newspaper or a folded cloth on the table. Hit it again as hard as before — but through the newspaper or cloth. Listen to how the newspaper or cloth stops some of the vibrations and makes the sound softer.

Strike various objects with the same ruler or pencil. Try a book, a metal doorknob, a sweater, the kitchen sink, a rug, and the bare floor. The hard things sound louder because they vibrate more than the soft things.

Scientists measure the loudness of a sound in *decibels*. A sound that you can barely hear has a level of zero decibels. The louder the sound, the higher the decibel level.

Here are the decibel levels for some familiar sounds:

Whisper – 20 decibels

Normal conversation – 60 decibels

Noisy school cafeteria – 80 decibels

Jet engine – 120 decibels

WONDER FACT: In 1982 there was a contest to find the person with the loudest voice. The winner was Susan Birmingham from Hong Kong. Her voice reached a level of 120 decibels!

Any sound above 120 decibels hurts the ear. Listening to loud sounds — over 90 decibels — for several hours can hurt your sense of hearing. Some rock concerts reach levels of more than 100 decibels. Such super-loud sounds can even cause deafness if a person is exposed to the sounds often enough.

Soundproofing and Echoes

As sound waves move through the air they bump into many different objects. Some are soft — like curtains, rugs, upholstered furniture, and clothing. These soft surfaces take in, or absorb, the sound waves. They soak up sound just as sponges soak up water. The more soft surfaces in the room, the softer the sound.

Noisy places, such as airplane cabins, factories, and school cafeterias, need more than soft surfaces to control the sound. They also need special *acoustical* tiles on the walls and ceiling. These tiles are made of soft materials that contain many small holes that trap and absorb the sound waves.

WONDER FACT: The quietest room in the world is the "Dead Room" at Bell Telephone Laboratories. All four walls, the ceiling, and the floor are covered with huge wedges of foam rubber. It is so quiet in the "Dead Room" that you can hear your heart beating and the blood flowing through your veins!

Sound waves also bump into hard things — such as walls, floors, ceilings, and closed windows. These surfaces bounce the sound waves back. The sound is reflected just like light from a mirror. Lots of hard surfaces in a room make sounds seem louder.

When sounds bounce off hard surfaces, you sometimes hear the same sound twice. You hear it first when the sound is made. Then you hear it again when it bounces back. The repeat is called an *echo*.

Shout your name in a quiet gymnasium. Clap your hands in a tiled bathroom. Make a loud noise facing a rocky cliff. Each time you'll hear the sound bounce back as an echo.

Whales use underwater echoes to find objects in the sea. The whale makes a sound. Then it listens for the echo. If the sound bounces back quickly, the whale knows something is nearby. If it takes a long time, the whale knows the object is far away.

Bats use sound and echoes the same way whales do. But the sound travels through air, not water.

WONDER FACT: Bats have an amazing sense of hearing. They can hear their sounds bounce off something as small as a tiny insect in flight. And then they fly fast enough to catch that insect.

High and Low

Sounds are either high or low in pitch. A squeaky door, a flute, and a crying baby are *high-pitched* sounds. Thunder, a bass fiddle, and a lion's roar are *low-pitched* sounds.

You can produce high and low pitches. Sing the very highest note that you can reach. Now let your voice slide all the way down. And then sing a low, growly note. Do you hear the difference in pitch?

Pitch depends on the speed of vibrations. The faster the vibrations, the higher the pitch. The slower the vibrations, the lower the pitch.

A high whistle has fast vibrations. A deep gong has slow vibrations.

Hold your hand lightly on the front of your throat. Sing a high note. Next, sing a low note. Did you feel the difference between the fast and slow vibrations?

Rubber bands work much like vocal cords. Stretch a rubber band very tight. Pluck it. The tight rubber band vibrates very fast. It makes a high sound.

Now let the rubber band become looser. Pluck it again. A loose rubber band vibrates more slowly. It produces a low pitch.

Frequency is another word for the speed of vibration. It tells you how fast something is vibrating. High frequencies produce high pitches. Low frequencies produce low pitches.

WONDER FACT: Humans can sing notes with frequencies from 60 vibrations per second to 4,000 vibrations per second. When singers hit very high, very loud notes, the vibrations may actually shatter glass.

WONDERS OF LIGHT

The world is filled with light.

Most of the light on earth comes from the sun. Indoors, light also comes from electric lamps. With both kinds of light we can see things outdoors, as well as in our homes, schools, and other indoor places.

What Is Light?

Light is a form of energy. It is the form of energy that lets us see. Light moves through the air as beams, or rays, or waves. It moves like waves through water. But light waves are super-super-fast!

WONDER FACT: Light travels at the speed of 186,000 miles a *second*! Nothing in the entire universe can move faster than a beam of light.

The sun is about 93 million miles from earth. If we could send a space shuttle to the sun today, it would take over 240 days to get there. Yet it takes a beam of sunlight only about eight minutes to reach earth!

The sun is a star. It is one of many stars. But the sun is much, much closer to earth than all the others. The rest are trillions and trillions of miles away.

All the stars are in the sky during the day, just as they are at night, but you can't see them when the sun is shining. The sun's light is too bright. You must wait until the sun sets. When it is dark you can see other stars.

WONDER FACT: **The sun shines on the earth as brightly as 2.5 billion, billion, billion candles.**

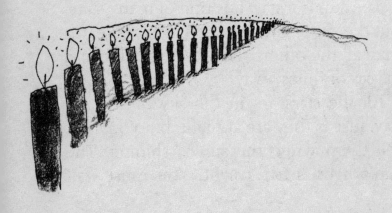

All stars shine. But none look as bright to us as the sun. That's because they are so very far away. The greater the distance from the earth, the dimmer the light from the star.

Scientists can measure how much light comes from each star. The brightness helps them to know exactly how far the star is from the earth.

WONDER FACT: **Next to the sun, the closest star system to earth is Alpha Centauri. It is nearly 26 trillion — that's 26,000,000,000,000 — miles away.**

An easy way to describe the distance from earth to the stars is by *light-years*. A light-year is the distance that light travels in one year.

You know that light travels 186,000 miles a second. In a year it travels about 6 trillion miles. So we say, "Alpha Centauri is 4⅓ light-years away." It tells us that the light we see from Alpha Centauri today left the star 4⅓ years ago!

WONDER FACT: The farthest stars that we can see are about 16 billion light-years away. They are so far away that we cannot see single stars. We see them with billions of other stars, in *galaxies.*

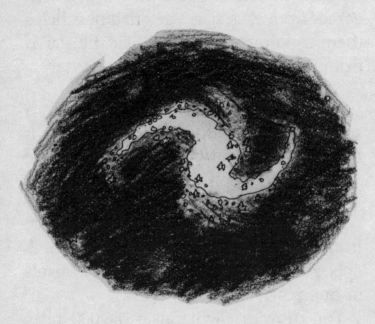

Because light travels so fast, it feels like it takes no time at all. Suppose you're at one end of a football field. Someone flashes a light at the other end. You see the light in about one ten millionth of a second.

Light travels much faster than sound. You probably know that the crash of thunder occurs at the same time as the flash of lightning. Yet you always see the lightning *before* you hear the thunder.

Sources of Light

At night and indoors we have to make our own light. In the old days people used fire and candles. For the last hundred years or so we have used electric light bulbs.

WONDER FACT: The oldest bulb still in use is in the firehouse at Livermore, California. It has been there since 1901. And it still gives off light!

But how do electric light bulbs work?

You flip the light switch. Electricity flows through wires into the bulb and out again. Inside the bulb is a short length of very thin wire. It is too skinny to carry the flow of electricity easily. The electricity squeezes and pushes its way through this wire.

As the electricity forces its way through, the wire gets very, very hot. It quickly glows white hot. And you see the white-hot glow as light!

Actually bulbs waste a lot of electric power. Most of the power goes to make the wire hot. Hold your hand near a light bulb while it's on. Careful! The bulb is too hot to touch. Only a small part of the electricity — about 5 percent — goes to produce light. The rest becomes heat.

Fluorescent tubes are more efficient than bulbs. The tubes produce less heat and more light. That's why you see mostly fluorescent lights in schools, stores, offices, and factories.

Here's how a fluorescent light works: Machines coat the inside of the glass tube with special chemicals and they fill the tube with a gas. When electricity passes through the gas in the tube, the chemicals on the inside start to glow. The glow produces the light.

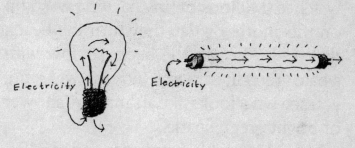

INCANDESCENT   FLUORESCENT

Did you know that a few living creatures make their own light? In summer, fireflies send out short flashes of light. They produce the light by mixing together different chemicals inside their bodies.

The railroad worm of South America actually glows in two colors! The worm is about three inches long. On its front and rear ends are bright red lights. Along its body are several shiny green spots.

When it crawls along, the railroad worm seems to be a tiny toy train. The red lights look like signal lights. And the green spots along its length look like lit windows.

A dazzling show of natural light is seen every September along certain California beaches. Millions of tiny bacteria wash up on the shore. By day they turn the beach dark red. At night the bacteria glow with a pale green light. If you kick the wet sand, you see what looks like an amazing shower of bright green sparks.

The sun and other stars, fire and candles, light bulbs and fluorescent tubes, fireflies and railroad worms — all give off their own light. But most objects — like books and bananas, hats and houses, cars and cats — do not make their own light. You can only see them if there is an outside source of light.

WONDER FACT: Fireflies use their light to find mates. Male fireflies follow the flashing lights of the females.

How We See

Right now you're reading this book. That means that light is shining on the page. Where is the light coming from? Is it sunlight? Or is it electric light?

The light strikes the book. It bounces back off the page.

Some of the light enters your eyes. It forms an upside down picture of the page on the back of your eyeball.

The picture on the back of your eyeball causes electrical signals to shoot to your brain. Your brain changes the signals into a right-side-up picture. You recognize it as a book. And you can read the words that are printed there.

Light that bounces off something is called *reflected light*. One of the best light reflectors is a mirror.

You can try this out: Aim a small mirror at a bright window or an electric light. Wiggle the mirror.

Do you see a point of light dancing around the room? The mirror reflects the light from the window or electric light and bounces it all around.

WONDER FACT: Mirrors can make light turn around and change direction.

Most mirrors are flat pieces of glass. Behind the glass is a thin layer of a shiny metal. Light passes through the glass. It strikes the metal. The metal reflects back the light. That's why you see your face when you look at a mirror.

Light surfaces reflect more light than dark surfaces. You are able to read this book because the printed words don't reflect as much light as the blank parts of the pages. The printed words only reflect about 3 percent of the light that falls on them. But the white paper of this book reflects about 85 percent of the light. That makes the letters look black.

Since black letters reflect only 3 percent of the light, what happens to the rest of the light?

The light that is *not* reflected is actually taken in, or *absorbed*, by the dark letters.

Here's a test you can try. Get two empty margarine or cottage cheese containers. Paint one container and lid white; paint the other black.

Fill the two containers almost to the top with water. Snap on the lids and place both containers in the freezer part of your refrigerator. Leave them there overnight.

The next day you'll see that the water has frozen into solid ice. Set the two containers side by side in a sunny spot. After an hour, see which container of ice has melted faster.

The black container probably has more melted water because the dark container absorbs more of the sun's light. Less ice melted in the white container because it reflected back more of the sunlight.

36

Light Bends and Turns

Light usually travels through air. But light also passes through glass or clear plastic. Such materials are *transparent*. You can see right through transparent materials. When you look through a window or through eyeglasses you are looking through transparent glass.

Window glass is usually flat. But the glass in eyeglasses is usually curved. A piece of curved glass is called a *lens*.

Something very strange happens when light passes through a lens. The lens bends the light.

The lenses used in eyeglasses and contact lenses, in microscopes and telescopes help people to see better. The lens in your camera allows you to take clear pictures of objects both near and far.

You can make light bend without a lens. Stand a long pencil in a half-filled glass of water. Look at the pencil from the side. It looks broken. That's because the light waves bend as they pass from the water, through the glass, and to your eye.

Here's a way to fool a friend by bending light. Ask someone, "Do you think a penny can float?" The answer will probably be, "No."

Drop a penny in a small bowl that you can't see through. Tell your friend to raise the bowl until the penny just disappears from sight. Now slowly pour water into the bowl. Surprise! The penny seems to "float" into view.

Light bends as it passes to your friend's eyes from the water. That's what makes the penny look like it is floating.

Shadows

Clouds, frosted glass, and thin sheets of paper let some — but not all — light through. Such materials are called *translucent*. Electric light bulbs and lamp shades are usually made of translucent materials.

Some other materials do not let any light through at all. We say these materials are *opaque*. Metal and wood, heavy cloth and cardboard, rocks and colored plastic are all opaque. Light cannot pass through opaque objects.

Can you guess what happens when you put an opaque object in front of a bright light? It casts a *shadow*. Shadow is the darkness behind something that is in the light.

All around us there are shadows. Clouds cast shadows on mountains. Trees and buildings make shadows on the ground. Wherever there is light and an opaque object, there is a shadow.

WONDER FACT: The largest shadows of all occur in space. They cause what we call *eclipses*.

SUN   EARTH   MOON

LUNAR ECLIPSE

SUN   MOON   EARTH

SOLAR ECLIPSE

Sometimes the earth comes between the sun and the moon. The earth casts a huge shadow that covers the moon. The moon seems to disappear. This is called a *lunar eclipse*.

Sometimes the moon comes between the sun and the earth. The moon casts a giant shadow on the earth. The sun seems to disappear. This is a *solar eclipse*.

You can make shadows anytime you like. Try this. In a dark room, shine a flashlight at a wall. Hold your hand in front of the flashlight. You'll see the shadow of your hand on the wall.

Your hand blocks some of the rays of light. That makes the shadow. The other light rays from the flashlight go past your hand. They make the bright area around the shadow.

Move your hand close to the flashlight. Watch the shadow grow larger.

Now stretch your hand out away from the flashlight. See how the shadow gets smaller.

Close to the flashlight your hand makes a big shadow. Farther away, the shadow is smaller.

WONDER FACT: The same object can make a long shadow or a short shadow.

In a dark room, stand a soda can or other opaque object on a light-colored table or desk. Shine a flashlight down from directly above the object. You'll see almost no shadow.

Now, keep aiming the light at the object. But slowly move the flashlight lower and lower along one side. Do you see the shadow growing longer and longer? When the flashlight is as low as the object, the shadow is as long as it can be.

Long and short shadows are easy to find on sunny days. Shadows are long in the morning when the sun is low in the sky. The shadows get shorter and shorter towards noon. At noon, the sun is almost directly overhead. That is when the shadows are shortest of all. As the sun sets, they get longer and longer.

Rainbows and Blue Skies

WONDER FACT: White light is made up of seven different colors.

The light from the sun looks white. But white light really contains the colors red, orange, yellow, green, blue, indigo, and violet. You can see these colors when something splits the white light apart.

Drops of rainwater can sometimes split white sunlight into its separate colors. When this happens you see a rainbow in the sky.

Diamonds, cut glass, bubbles, a spray of water from a fountain or hose, and a thin layer of oil also break light up into its separate colors.

If light is made up of seven colors, why is the sky blue?

Dust and drops of water are always in the air. They split the light from the sun into its different colors. The colors scatter across the sky.

The dust and water also change the direction of the different colors. Of all the colors, blue is bent the most. Blue light shines down on the earth. That's why the sky looks blue.

When the sun rises or sets, the color changes. More red and pink show up in the sky. That is because the light passes through more of the atmosphere when the sun is low.

You can make your own blue sky. Fill a glass with water. Add just a few drops of milk. Go to a dark room and shine a flashlight through the glass. Look into the glass from above.

The tiny drops of milk in the water scatter the blue part of the flashlight beam. It is much like dust and raindrops scattering the blue in the sunlight. The water looks slightly blue in color.

Lasers

In 1960, a new type of light was invented. It is called a *laser*. The laser is the brightest light that we have.

WONDER FACT: The light of some lasers is 1,000 times as bright as the sun. One look at a high-power laser can blind a person for life!

Laser light is different from ordinary light in two very important ways. The light rays that make up ordinary light leave the source at different times. And they go off every which way. Laser light rays all move together. They all go in one direction.

Think of the exit gate of a big stadium. It's the end of a football game. The fans pour out and head off in all directions. Some run. Some walk. Some are ahead of the crowd. Others are behind. That is like ordinary light.

Now think of a marching band coming out of the same gate. They are in step and all moving together at the same speed. That is like laser light.

As you know, ordinary white light is made up of all the colors of the rainbow. But laser light contains only one color.

Picture an ordinary flashlight beam on a dark night. The light spreads out. The beam only seems to reach a few dozen feet at most.

Not so with a laser beam. Lasers are very sharp and narrow beams of light. They can shine over a very long distance. Their light barely spreads out at all.

WONDER FACT: A laser beam can reach up to the moon.

In 1962, scientists aimed a laser at the moon, 250,000 miles away. The laser made a circle of light on the moon that could be seen from the earth. But because the laser spread so little, the circle was only 2½ miles across!

You may not know it, but lasers are at work all around you. Supermarkets have them. The checkout clerk slides an item over an opening in the counter. A small laser inside "reads" the zebralike black-and-white lines on the package. The name and price of the item print out on a strip of paper.

People use lasers to play CDs. The CD, or compact disc, is a metal-coated plastic disc, covered on one side with tiny, tiny spots and pits. As the disc spins around inside the CD player, a laser "reads" the spots and pits. It changes them into vibrations, which produce the sounds you hear.

WONDER FACT: Laser beams can carry telephone conversations through thin glass fibers.

The lasers flash quickly on and off to carry a message through a glass fiber. The fibers used for laser communication are quite amazing. Each one is less than half as thick as a hair on your head. Yet they are twice as strong as steel of the same thickness. And each fiber can carry up to 350 telephone conversations at the same time!

Doctors use the heat and the sharp point of lasers to operate on the eye, ear, throat, and other parts of the body. Soldiers use lasers to aim their guns and missiles. Factory workers use lasers for everything from cutting holes in baby bottle nipples to welding pieces of metal together to measuring the sizes of different parts of an automobile engine.

We've come a long way from fire and candles to today's lasers. Some say the future will be even "brighter" as scientists learn even more about light and what it can do!

WONDERS OF WATER

Water is the most common substance on earth. It is found everywhere, in oceans, lakes, and rivers. In fact, 75 percent of the earth is covered with water!

WONDER FACT: Water is the only substance on the earth found as a liquid, solid, and gas.

Water is a liquid. A liquid feels soft. It does not have a shape of its own. In a glass, a liquid takes the shape of the glass.

In a bowl, it's the shape of the bowl. You can pour liquids from one container to another.

But suppose you put a dish of liquid water into the freezer part of your refrigerator. What happens? The water becomes ice. Ice is a *solid*. A solid feels hard. It has a definite shape.

Water freezes if it is below 32 degrees F (for Fahrenheit). It's below 32 degrees F in your freezer. And it's way below 32 degrees F at both the North and South Poles. All the water at the two poles is frozen solid. Rivers and lakes freeze whenever the temperature drops below 32 degrees F.

The third state of water is water vapor. Water vapor is a *gas*. The water vapor mixes in with the air, which is a mixture of gases.

You can't see or feel most gases. You can move your hand in a gas, and not feel anything. You can push against a gas, and nothing will push back. Gases don't have any fixed shape. They fill up any container.

Water can be a solid, liquid, and gas.

Pic 1. Place an ice cube on a paper towel.

Pic 2. In a few minutes the solid ice starts to melt. It becomes liquid water, which soaks into the paper towel.

Pic 3. Wipe the table with the wet paper towel. At first there's a damp spot. But as you watch, the spot grows smaller and smaller.

Pic 4. Finally, the water is all gone. It becomes a gas (water vapor) and goes into the air.

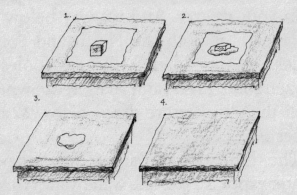

Condensation

Magicians make things appear from nothing. Would you like to do it, too? You can make water appear from thin air. Only it's not magic. It's one of the wonders of water!

Put some ice cubes in a clean, dry glass. Let the glass and ice cubes stand on a table for about 10 minutes.

Look at the outside of the glass. See how it has begun to "sweat." Little drops of liquid water cling to the sides.

What made the water appear? Where did it come from?

The air in the room is warmer than the cold glass. Like all air, the air in the room contains water vapor. And warm air holds more water vapor than cold air.

Some of the warm air in the room touched the cold glass. The warm air got chilled. It couldn't hold as much water vapor as before. The water vapor was forced out of the air. The vapor (an invisible gas) changed into water (a visible liquid). It showed up as drops of water on the cold glass.

The change from water vapor to liquid water is called *condensation*. Condensation happens when warm air is cooled.

WONDER FACT: Condensation makes water appear where there seemed to be none before.

You can see condensation all around you.

On cold days, your warm breath meets the chilly air. The water vapor in your breath condenses. It forms small drops of water in the air. The drops look like tiny clouds coming out of your mouth.

In warm weather, the sun heats the air during the day. The warm air holds a good deal of water vapor. After the sun sets, the land cools off. The water vapor in the air condenses. Liquid water appears. By morning the grass and other plants are wet with dew.

WONDER FACT: In places where there is little rain, dew can supply plants with all the water they need to grow.

Sometimes warm air flows over land or water that is cold. The warm air is cooled. The water vapor in the warm air condenses. It forms tiny drops of water. When this happens near the surface of the earth, we have fog. When it happens higher up in the air, there are clouds.

Evaporation

The next time you take a hot bath or shower, look at the bathroom mirror. Is it wet and foggy? The bath or shower warms the air in the bathroom. The warm air bumps into the cold mirror. The air gets chilled. This forces the water vapor out of the air. The vapor condenses. And droplets of water form on the mirror.

Later, when the air cools, the mirror gets clear again. The water is all gone. We say that the water has *evaporated*.

WONDER FACT: Evaporation makes water seem to disappear.

You've seen evaporation many times:

You wipe a table with a damp towel — and the table is soon dry.

You step out of a swimming pool — and get dry without using a towel.

You go for a walk after a summer rainstorm — and the streets are not even wet.

Where did the water go?

In each case, most of the water changed from liquid water, which you can see — to water vapor, which you can't see. The change is evaporation at work.

Warm water evaporates faster than cold water.

To see this happen, get two small, identical bowls. Put 2 teaspoons of tap water in each one. Place one bowl in the refrigerator. Place the second on a sunny windowsill or in some other warm spot.

Leave both bowls for a day. Then check them. Which has evaporated faster? Can you guess why?

Each day the heat of the sun evaporates water from every ocean, lake, and river in the world. About 85 percent of the water vapor in the air rises up from the earth's oceans alone.

WONDER FACT: When ocean water evaporates, the salt it contains does not evaporate. It stays in the ocean. That's why the ocean remains salty.

To learn more about ocean water, try this.

Pic 1. Add 6 tablespoons of salt to a glass of water and stir. The water is now salty like ocean water.

Pic 2. Pour some of the saltwater onto a plate. Leave it in a warm place until all the water has evaporated.

Pic 3. All that's left on the plate is a white powder. Taste it. It's salt. The water evaporated. But the salt did not.

1.   2.   3.

Dissolving

WONDER FACT: Water can make some substances disappear.

When water evaporates, it disappears. Water can also make other things disappear.

Your hands are dirty and you wash them in water. The dirt disappears.

You add sugar to lemonade. After you stir, you can't see the sugar.

Where do the dirt and the sugar go?

Water is made up of tiny, tiny bits called molecules. When something disappears in water its molecules fit in between the molecules of the water. We say that it dissolves.

Fill a measuring cup with exactly one cup of water. Stir in a teaspoon of sugar. Watch it dissolve.

You might expect that adding sugar to a cup of water makes the level of the water rise. Did it? Why not?

It didn't rise because the sugar fit in between the molecules of water. You still have one cup of water. No more. No less.

Water in Human Beings

Every living thing is made up mostly of water. Your blood is almost all water. And your skin, flesh, and organs all contain lots of water.

WONDER FACT: Seventy percent of the human body is water. If you weigh 80 pounds, 56 pounds are water!

The amount of water in your body must stay at a normal level. If not, you feel the difference. A slight drop and you feel thirsty.

Lose a little more and your body starts to change. Your skin begins to shrink and feel tight. It's hard to move your arms and legs. You can't think clearly.

A drop of 10 percent in body water may lead to death.

WONDER FACT: A person can live without food for more than a month. But no one can live for even one week without water.

Living beings need water to stay healthy. Water dissolves the chemicals in food that the body needs. And water carries the chemicals to all parts of the body. Finally, water washes away the body's wastes.

You need about 2½ quarts of water a day. No, you don't have to drink that much water daily! Milk, juice, and soda are almost all water. The rest comes from the solid foods you eat.

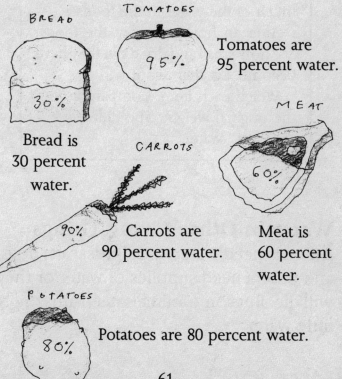

BREAD
30%
Bread is 30 percent water.

TOMATOES
95%
Tomatoes are 95 percent water.

CARROTS
90%
Carrots are 90 percent water.

MEAT
60%
Meat is 60 percent water.

POTATOES
80%
Potatoes are 80 percent water.

Here's how you can prove that food contains lots of water. On a kitchen scale weigh a slice of bread, a vegetable, and a piece of fruit one at a time. Jot down the exact weight of each one.

Place the three items in the oven. Ask an adult to set the oven at 200 degrees. Leave the items there for an hour. The heat of the oven will speed up the evaporation. It will drive out much of the water in the foods.

After an hour, take out the foods. See how small and dried out they have become. Let them cool.

Weigh each item. Compare it with the original weight. The difference is the "lost" water.

Water in Other Living Things

Animals need water, too. Birds, cats, dogs, and others need supplies of water or they will die. But some animals need amazingly little water.

WONDER FACT: Camels can live for a whole winter without a drop of water. In the summer, though, they need water after about five days.

Camels can survive a long time without drinking water for several reasons. They get some water from the plants they eat. They also produce some water from the fat in their own bodies. And since they hardly sweat at all, they lose almost no water through the skin.

Some people believe that the camel stores water in its hump. That's not true. The hump is all fat.

WONDER FACT: The kangaroo rat *never* drinks water.

The tiny desert animal called the kangaroo rat only eats seeds and other plants that grow in sand. All the water it needs comes from these foods.

The kangaroo rat also keeps most of the water it produces. It sweats very little. It spends the hottest part of each day motionless in a cool tunnel under the desert sand.

Most plants also need water. The water comes in through the roots. It passes to all the branches and leaves.

The plant needs the water to live and grow. Any water that the plant does not need passes out through tiny openings in the leaves. These openings are called *stomata*.

Some leaves have as many as a million stomata! Great amounts of water pass out through each of these leaves.

WONDER FACT: The leaves of just one birch tree give off about 70 gallons of water daily. An acre of corn plants gives off about 4,000 gallons of water a day! All of this water goes into the air as water vapor.

The Waters of the Earth

WONDER FACT: Clouds and rain are condensed water!

The water that evaporates from plants escapes into the air as water vapor. So does the water that evaporates from oceans and lakes and rivers around the world.

The water vapor is carried up by air. Higher and higher it goes.

Soon it reaches a level where the air is very cold. Do you remember what happens when warm air meets cold air? The water vapor in the warm air condenses. It forms tiny drops of liquid water. The drops come together in a cloud.

As time passes, the little drops of water come together. They form bigger and bigger drops of water. They also get heavier and heavier. Soon they are just too heavy to stay up in the air.

The drops of water fall to the earth. Rain comes pattering down on streets and fields, on rooftops, on ships at sea, on woods and forests, and on you!

WONDER FACT: Snowflakes are frozen water vapor.

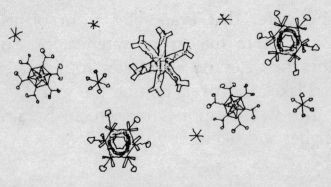

Sometimes the air up high is very, very cold. It is so cold that the water vapor freezes into a solid before it can condense into a liquid. It freezes into snowflakes. Then snow falls instead of rain.

Every snowflake is in the form of a crystal. And each one has exactly six sides. Yet no two snowflakes are exactly the same!

If you live where it is cold, you can see this for yourself. Take a dark piece of paper or cardboard outside when it is snowing. Wait for the paper to get cold. Then catch some snowflakes on it.

Look at the snowflakes. You may need a magnifying glass to see them clearly. Count the six sides. Find the differences among them.

When next it rains or snows, think of this: The water on the earth is always evaporating. It goes up into the air as water vapor. Some of the water vapor turns into clouds and falls to the earth as rain. Some of the water vapor freezes and falls to the earth as snow.

The water just keeps going around and around. No water is ever lost. The earth's supply of water never gets used up.

WONDER FACT: Every glassful of water you drink contains trillions and trillions of molecules. These molecules are millions of years old. It is quite possible that George Washington gulped down one of the same water molecules some 200 years ago!

WONDERS OF HEAT

What Makes Things Hot or Cold?

Objects are hot when they have lots of heat energy. Objects are cold when they have little heat energy. To change something from cold to hot, you need to add heat energy.

You can add heat energy to objects in several ways. One way is to put the object near something that has lots of heat energy.

Let's say you want to heat a pot of cold water. You put the pot on the stove and turn on the gas or electricity. The burner gives off lots of heat energy. The energy moves to the water. And the water gets hot.

Another way to add heat energy is by rubbing. Hold your two hands together. Feel how warm — or cold — they are. Now rub your hands against each other. Use lots of force. Rubbing your hands together creates heat energy and makes them feel toasty warm.

Can you think of another way to create heat by rubbing?

WONDER FACT: The American Indians knew that you can start a fire by rubbing two dry sticks of wood together. They rubbed them very hard and fast. The rubbing made fine wood dust. When the dust became hot enough, it began to burn. The Indians then used the burning dust to start their fire.

Pressing on things can make them hot, too. The pressure adds heat energy in the form of heat.

You use the heat made by pressure when you ice skate. Your body's weight rests on the blades of your ice skates. The blades press down hard on the ice. The pressure heats the ice. The top of the ice melts and for an instant becomes water. And you skate — or slide — through the water!

You can see how pressure builds up heat. Get an ice cube and a fork. Press the fork down hard on the ice cube. Hold it there for a minute or two. Then take it away. The fork leaves a mark where the pressure melted the ice cube!

Rubbing and pressing are two ways to make something hot. Stretching is still another method.

Find a large, thick rubber band. Hold it loosely against your lips. Notice how cool it feels.

With the rubber band still against your lips, quickly pull your hands apart. Stretch the rubber band as fast and as far as you can.

Do you feel the rubber band get warmer? The sudden stretching adds heat energy to the rubber band!

Heat Flows

Everyone knows that water flows. But did you know that heat flows, too? You can't see heat flowing, but you can see the results.

Put a few ice cubes into a glass of tap water. What makes the water get colder? Heat flows out of the water and into the ice cubes.

For proof, just look at the ice cubes. They are becoming smaller. The heat from the water is melting the ice cubes!

Try this the next time you have a cup of cocoa that is too hot to drink. Put a spoon into the cup. The heat from the hot cocoa flows into the cold spoon. That helps to cool the cocoa. In a minute or two it is just right for drinking.

Now touch the spoon. It feels warm. The heat from the cocoa warms up the spoon.

Heat also flows within your body. The inside of your body is always warm. But on cold days, some of the heat flows out into the cold air and you feel cold.

On hot days you feel very hot. That makes you perspire. The perspiration speeds up the flow of heat out of your body when it evaporates. And the rapid flow of heat helps to keep you cool.

When you are sick, your temperature sometimes goes up. You have a *fever*.

To find out if you have a fever, your parents take your temperature. They use a thermometer. A thermometer measures heat. If your body is hotter than 98.6 degrees F, you are probably ill.

Sometimes the body fights off the illness all by itself. The fever disappears in a day or two. Other times the doctor prescribes medicine to treat the sickness and bring down the fever.

WONDER FACT: The highest temperature a human ever reached was 110 degrees F. The lowest was 61 degrees F! Both patients survived.

Not all animals have the same body temperature.

Goats have a normal body temperature of 102.8 degrees F.

Cats and dogs have normal body temperatures between 100 and 102.5 degrees F.

Horses have a normal body temperature between 99 and 100.5 degrees F.

When the golden hamster is hibernating it has the lowest temperature of all — 38.3 degrees F!

Heat Expands

Have you ever noticed —

- that sidewalks and roads have lines cut into them?
- that there are small spaces between lengths of railroad track?
- that there are gaps between sections of bridges?

Do you know why?

WONDER FACT: Heat makes most things grow bigger.

When something grows bigger we say it *expands*. Solids, liquids, and gases usually expand as they get hot.

The concrete of sidewalks and roads also expands in the summer heat. When the concrete has no room to expand, it buckles and cracks.

Railroad tracks and bridges are made of metal. The spaces between sections of track or bridge provide room for the metal to expand in hot weather.

Liquids also expand when they are heated. You can see this in a thermometer. Most thermometers have a thin column of liquid on the inside. When the liquid gets hot, it expands. It moves up the tube. The height of the liquid tells you the temperature.

Gases, too, take up more space when they are heated. You can see this for yourself. Get a clean, empty bottle with a narrow neck, a balloon, and a pan partly filled with water.

Stretch the opening of the balloon over the neck of the bottle. Set the bottle in the pan and put the pan on the stove. Ask an adult to heat the water in the pan.

Watch the balloon. At first it droops down to one side. But in a few minutes it pops up, just as though someone blew it up!

Here's what happened: First, the heat from the stove warmed the water in the pan. The heat flowed to the air inside the bottle. As the air became warm, it expanded. It needed more space. Since there was no more room in the bottle, some of the air moved up into the balloon. And the balloon filled up with air!

WONDER FACT: Rockets, jet planes, and automobiles are all powered by hot, expanding gases.

Rockets, jet planes, and automobiles all burn fuel. The burning fuel produces a gas. The gas is hot. It expands. The gas pushes the rocket or jet plane forward. It flies into space or through the air.

In the automobile the gas pushes against pistons. As they move up and down in the engine, they power the car.

Heat Can Travel

You probably know that heat can travel great distances. The best example is the heat from the sun. The sun warms the earth — from a distance of about 93 million miles!

WONDER FACT: The temperature on the outside of the sun is a scorching 11,000 degrees F! But the temperature inside the sun is even hotter — 30 million degrees F.

The sun shines on the whole earth. But not all places get warmed evenly. Some spots get too much heat. Some spots do not get enough heat.

WONDER FACT: The hottest place on earth is Libya in Africa. The temperature can be as high as 136.4 degrees F in the shade. The coldest spot is near the South Pole. The record is 128.9 degrees F below zero.

As the earth spins, each spot is in the sunlight for part of the time. During those hours it is day. Each spot is also dark for part of the time. That is when it is night.

It is always warmer during the day when the sun is shining. And it is usually colder at night.

WONDER FACT: The biggest day-to-night change in temperature was in Browning, Montana, on January 23, 1916. The temperature was 44 degrees F during the day. But it dropped to 56 degrees below zero F at night. That's a difference of 100 degrees!

Heat rays are like rays of light — except that you can't see them. But you sure can feel them! They come out of any hot object.

Stand near a fire — and you feel the heat rays.

Hold your hand over a hot oven — and you feel the heat rays.

Stay outdoors on a sunny summer day — and you really feel the heat rays.

On cold winter days, the heaters in your house send out heat rays. They keep you warm.

But most heaters are small. How do they heat a whole house or apartment?

Heat waves from the heater warm the cold air around the heater.

The warm air floats up above the cold air.

The cold air is pushed down and is heated.

Round and round the air moves — hot air rising, cold air falling.

Why does hot air rise and cold air fall?

WONDER FACT: Hot air weighs less than cold air.

You recall that heat makes things grow bigger, or expand. Air, too, expands when it is heated.

Here are two identical balloons. They are both filled with the exact same amount of air. They are the same size.

Suppose one balloon is heated. The heat makes the air inside expand. This balloon becomes bigger than the other.

How can you make the hot balloon the same size as the cold balloon? Let some air out of the hot balloon.

What if the balloons were weighed now? The hot balloon now contains less air than the cold balloon. Therefore, the hot balloon would weigh less than the cold one. This shows that hot air weighs less than cold air.

You can actually watch the hot air rising in a room. Take a piece of paper about 5 inches square. Starting from the center, draw a spiral like a snail shell. The curves should be about a half inch apart. Let the spiral fill the whole paper.

From the outside in, cut along the spiral line. Thread a needle and pass the thread through the center of the spiral. Tie a knot underneath. Remove the needle and carry the spiral by the thread.

Now walk around the room. Hold your spiral over a heater, the stove, a lamp — even a bowl of hot soup! Watch the rising hot air make your spiral spin.

Heat also moves through liquids and through solid objects. Watch someone place a pot of soup on a hot stove. The stove heats only the bottom of the pot. Yet, the heat moves through the solid pot and heats the liquid soup. And soon the soup is bubbly hot.

But not all solids carry heat equally well. Take wood, for example. When someone lights a wooden match, one end is on fire. Yet the person can hold the other end without burning his or her fingers.

Cooks use a wooden spoon to stir spaghetti in a pot of boiling water. The part touching the spaghetti gets very hot. But the handle remains cool.

Heat does not move easily through cloth. That's one reason you wear clothing. Clothes stop your body heat from escaping. At the same time they stop the cold from getting in.

On very cold days, it's a good idea to wear several layers of clothing. Each layer of clothing helps to hold in your body heat.

The layers of clothing also trap layers of air. Air doesn't carry heat very well, either. Several layers of air can keep in the warmth and keep out the cold better than one layer.

Using Heat

As you know, every drop of water is made up of billions and billions of tiny bits called molecules. The molecules are always in motion. In cold water, they move around a little bit. In hot water they dash and dart about at high speed.

You can't see water molecules. But you can prove that hot molecules move more than cold molecules.

Pour very hot water in one glass. Pour very cold water in another glass. Carefully put one drop of food coloring into each glass. Watch what happens.

In the hot water, the food coloring quickly spreads all around. It soon colors all the water.

In the cold water, the food coloring doesn't spread as fast. It takes a long time for the water to be colored.

The reason is that the molecules of hot water are jumping and scooting around. They push the molecules of food coloring in all directions. The water quickly changes color.

The molecules of cold water are not as active. They don't push the food coloring around as much. So the color spreads more slowly.

When water is put on a hot stove, the molecules leap about madly.

Some molecules have so much heat energy that they pop up out of the water as steam.

The steam mixes in with the air and disappears.

When water is put in a freezer, the molecules hardly move at all.

The molecules lock tightly in place and the water freezes.

The liquid water becomes a solid piece of ice.

WONDERS OF AIR

Have you ever said —
- this box is empty?
- there's nothing in that bottle?
- that log is hollow?

The box, the bottle, and the log may have looked empty. But they were not empty at all. They were full of air!

WONDER FACT: Air is everywhere around us. It fills all the places and spaces that look empty.

How can we prove that there is air in "empty" places?

Get a tall "empty" glass. Crumple a tissue. Push the tissue tightly into the bottom of the glass. Hold the glass upside down. Press it straight down all the way into a big bowl of water.

Hold it there for a moment. Then pick the glass straight up. Take out the tissue. The tissue is completely dry!

Why?

There was air in the "empty" glass. The air kept the water out of the bottom of the glass. So the tissue didn't get wet!

What Is Air?

For thousands of years, everyone believed that air was one simple substance. Then about 200 years ago, scientists found that air is made up of several gases. The most important gases in air are nitrogen and oxygen.

Nitrogen makes up nearly 80 percent of the air. You breathe in nitrogen every time you take a breath. But your body does not need this gas. So you breathe it right out again.

Along with the nitrogen, you also breathe in oxygen. Oxygen makes up about 20 percent of the air. Every human and every animal needs oxygen in order to live.

WONDER FACT: People can live more than a month without food. They can live about a week without water. But they can live only about ten minutes without oxygen.

Take a deep breath. Hold it. Look at a clock or watch. How long can you keep in your breath? Most people can go for about one minute without breathing.

Besides nitrogen, oxygen, and some other gases, air also contains tiny bits of dust. Dust is made up of specks of sand, cloth, metal, wood, plastic, ash, hair, and many other materials. They enter the air in three main ways: when things rub against each other, when fires burn, and when strong winds blow.

Dust is always floating in the air. That's because the dust particles are so very light. But it's hard to see the dust in the air.

Here's one way to see dust. Shine a flashlight in a dark room. The beam will show up the tiny bits of dust in the air.

WONDER FACT: Dust bits are so tiny that a row of 50,000 dust bits would only measure about one inch.

Each time you take a breath, the air passes through your nose. Inside your nose are tiny hairs. The hairs catch some of the dust that is in the air. Sometimes there is lots of dust in the air. It piles up on the hairs. Kachoo! The dust makes you sneeze.

WONDER FACT: The hairs in your nose catch about a pound of dust in a year.

From your nose the air passes through a tube called your *trachea*, or windpipe. The trachea carries the air to your lungs.

Very thin blood vessels surround your lungs. The oxygen in the air passes through the walls of the lungs and into the blood vessels. Then the blood carries the oxygen all over your body. The oxygen helps your body produce the heat and energy you need to live and grow.

Most fuels — coal, oil, and wood — need oxygen in order to burn. Burning uses up some of the oxygen in the air.

Attach a small birthday candle to a bit of wood. Float the wood — with the candle — on about one inch of water in a bowl. Ask a grownup to light the candle.

Hold a large drinking glass upside down over the burning candle. Lower the glass so the rim of the glass is in the water. Notice how high the water comes in the glass.

As the candle burns, the level of the water in the glass rises. It takes the place of the oxygen that is used up. As soon as all the oxygen is gone, the candle flame goes out.

Look at the new level of the water. It is higher than before.

Air Presses in All Directions

The earth is surrounded by a thick, thick blanket of air. It weighs down on the land and sea. It covers everything on earth.

The air presses down with a great deal of force. On every square inch of surface there is a weight of nearly 15 pounds!

You can test the weight of the air this way. Get a slat of wood about the length and thickness of a yardstick. Place it on a table. Leave about 3 inches sticking out over the table edge.

Cover the slat with two sheets of a large-size newspaper. Smooth out the paper. Stroke it from the center out to the edges.

About 5 tons of air are pressing down on the paper. They hold the slat firmly on the table.

Now hit the end of the slat very hard with a hammer. The weight of the air keeps the slat from moving. Instead of flipping up, the slat breaks!

WONDER FACT: The air presses on your body with a weight of about 15 tons — the weight of ten automobiles!

How can you walk around under the weight of ten automobiles?

You're able to walk because your body presses out just as hard as the air presses in. The pressure inside and the pressure outside are exactly the same. They are in balance. So you don't feel the outside force.

WONDER FACT: Air doesn't only press down. It also presses up and to the sides.

Hold out your hand. The weight of the air pressing down on your hand is about 100 pounds. Why doesn't the weight push your hand down?

The upward pressure of the air keeps your hand in the air. The ↑ pressure equals the ↓ pressure.

You can use the upward pressure of air to do a magic trick.

Cut a piece of thin cardboard or an index card slightly bigger than the top of a small glass. Fill the glass to the very top with water. Cover the top with the cardboard or index card.

Hold the cover tightly on the glass with your hand. Now, slowly tip the glass upside down. Do this over a sink. Then carefully slide your hand away.

Does the water pour out? No! The cover stays in place!

Why?

The air is pressing up on the cover. The pressure is more than the weight of the water pressing down. The upward pressure keeps the water in the glass!

How Air Moves

Whenever warm air meets cold air, the cold air pushes up the warm air.

You know how a heater warms a room. The heater heats the air around it. The heated air expands and becomes lighter. It rises.

The cool, heavy air in the room sinks down. When the cold air reaches the heater, it also becomes warm. And it, too, is pushed up.

Round and round, the air keeps moving. This moving air is really wind.

Look around and you can see how hot air makes a wind.

Find a smoking chimney. The fire heats the air in the chimney. The smoke is carried up by the hot air rising from the fire.

Look at the air above a pot when water is boiling. The hot air wind rises and takes the steam with it.

WONDER FACT: The sun makes winds blow outdoors.

The hot sun warms the air. But the sun doesn't heat the air evenly. The air in some places gets very hot. It rises. Cooler air rushes in to take its place. And the wind blows.

The strongest winds come during storms. Of all storms, hurricanes are the worst. Powerful winds blow. Drenching rains fall. Hurricane winds and rain do tremendous damage to everything in their wide path.

Tornados are also very dangerous. Their winds are even more powerful than hurricane winds. But they follow a very narrow path — less than 1,000 feet wide — and they stay in one place only for about 30 seconds. Tornado winds take on a shape like a funnel, with the point facing down. This point, though, can knock over buildings and pick up heavy cars as though they were toys!

WONDER FACT: The winds in a hurricane blow at speeds of more than 75 miles an hour. The winds in tornados may reach 300 miles an hour.

TORNADO

Air Around the Earth

Planet Earth is surrounded by a blanket of air. This cover of air is called the *atmosphere*. As the earth moves through space, the atmosphere moves with it. The atmosphere is held to the earth by gravity.

The air is thickest at the surface of the earth. A thick blanket is warmer than a thin one. Valleys and other low places have the whole thickness of the blanket of air to keep them warm.

The higher you go, the thinner the air. A mountaintop has a very thin blanket of air above it. That is one reason why mountains are colder than lowlands.

The air is even thinner high above the mountains. Fly in an airplane and you pass through air that is very thin indeed. Fly in a space shuttle and you reach the very top of the atmosphere. At about 1,000 miles above the earth you are at the beginning of outer space.

The earth's atmosphere contains the air we need to breathe. But the atmosphere helps us in another way. It shields us from stone and metal particles from outer space. These particles are known as meteors. When meteors land on the earth they are called meteorites. The earth is always being struck by meteorites.

WONDER FACT: About 100 billion meteorites strike the earth every day.

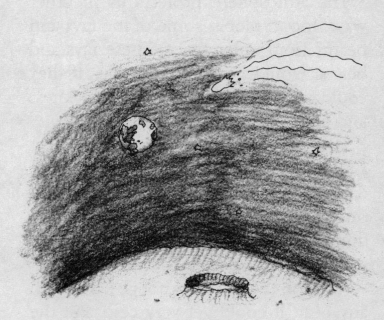

Most meteorites are tiny. They look like little grains of sand. But some are huge. They are like giant rocks. If a large meteorite fell on a city it would kill many people.

Few big meteors reach the earth. As they pass through the atmosphere they rub against the air. The air breaks up the big ones. It wears them away. Finally, the falling meteors are nothing more than harmless specks of dust.

The atmosphere protects us in other ways, too. It blocks some of the rays and beams from outer space. These rays and beams would be very dangerous if they could reach us. They would cause sickness and death.

The atmosphere also keeps the earth at a comfortable temperature. During the day, heat rays from the sun pour down on earth. The heat could damage living things. But the atmosphere holds back some of the heat from the sun's rays.

At night, the sun does not give the earth any heat. It could get very cold. But the atmosphere traps some of the day's heat. The trapped heat makes us feel warmer at night.

WONDER FACT: The atmosphere has four separate layers.

The bottom layer of the atmosphere is called the *troposphere*. About 80 percent of all the air of the atmosphere is in the troposphere. All the weather is found here, too. The winds, storms, rain, and snow are in the troposphere. The air at this level contains lots of water vapor and dust, as well.

Above the troposphere is the *stratosphere*. It extends up about 20 miles from the troposphere. There is no weather in the stratosphere. That is why jetliners fly there. The air is much thinner at this height.

On top of the stratosphere is the *mesosphere*. Here the air is very thin. Meteor trails can be seen in the mesosphere.

The fourth layer is called the *thermosphere*.

This layer continues into outer space. The lower part of the thermosphere is called the ionosphere. The ionosphere reflects back radio waves.

A radio station sends out a signal. The signal reaches the ionosphere. It bounces back to earth. Back and forth the signal races. In a flash, it can speed around the entire world.

The ionosphere does not reflect television signals. To send a television signal a long distance you need a satellite. The satellite receives the signal beamed up from the television station. And it bounces the signal back down to earth.

Compressed Air

Air can be squeezed. It can be forced into a small space. Air that is squeezed into a small space is called *compressed air*.

WONDER FACT: You can lift a heavy book with compressed air.

Place a balloon near the edge of a table. Let the neck of the balloon hang over the side. Put a book on top of the balloon.

Now blow into the balloon. Blow very hard. You have to compress the air inside the balloon.

Watch the book at the same time. You'll see it rise up off the table. The compressed air in the balloon is strong enough to lift the book!

Every time you bounce a ball, you use compressed air. The ball is filled with air. As the ball hits the ground, it gets pushed in on one side. This compresses the air. The compressed air pushes out on the same side. And the ball bounces up.

WONDER FACT: **The compressed air in automobile tires holds up cars that weigh thousands of pounds.**

The service station lifts that pick up automobiles work on compressed air.

The compressed air in air
hammers breaks up concrete.

The pump you use to blow
up a football or a bicycle tire uses
compressed air.

Air is at work all around you!

It keeps you alive.

It holds up giant airplanes.

It powers sailboats and windmills.

Heat the air — and it can warm up a whole house.

Squeeze the air — and it can hold up an automobile.

You can't see it or smell it. But air is vital to our lives!